I0813984

Intro to Spanish

Bela Davis

Español

Abdo Kids Junior
is an Imprint of Abdo Kids
abdobooks.com

Abdo
INTRO TO LANGUAGE
Kids

abdobooks.com

Published by Abdo Kids, a division of ABDO, P.O. Box 398166, Minneapolis, Minnesota 55439.

Printed in China

102023

012024

Consultant: Maria Puchol

Photo Credits: Getty Images, Shutterstock

Production Contributors: Teddy Borth, Jennie Forsberg, Grace Hansen

Design Contributors: Candice Keimig, Colleen McLaren

Library of Congress Control Number: 2023937679

Publisher's Cataloging-in-Publication Data

Names: Davis, Bela, author.

Title: Intro to Spanish / by Bela Davis

Description: Minneapolis, Minnesota : Abdo Kids, 2024 | Series: Intro to language | Includes online resources and index.

Identifiers: ISBN 9781098268336 (lib. bdg.) | ISBN 9781098269036 (ebook) | ISBN 9781098269388 (Read-to-Me ebook)

Subjects: LCSH: Spanish language--Juvenile literature. | Informal language learning--Juvenile literature. | Language and languages--Juvenile literature. | Bilingual books--Juvenile literature.

Classification: DDC 418.00--dc23

Table of Contents

Intro to Spanish

Spanish is spoken around the world. Let's learn some words!

Spanish	bienvenido
English	welcome

North America
Europe
Spain
Africa
South America
N
E
S
W
Spanish is an official language

uno

one

dos

two

seis

six

siete

seven

tres
three

cuatro
four

cinco
five

ocho
eight

nueve
nine

diez
ten

once

eleven

doce

twelve

dieciséis

sixteen

diecisiete

seventeen

trece
thirteen

catorce
fourteen

quince
fifteen

dieciocho
eighteen

diecinueve
nineteen

veinte
twenty

colores
colors
naranja
orange
amarillo
yellow
rojo
red
blanco
white

verde
green
azul
blue
morado
purple
negro
black

hola

hello

adiós

goodbye

buenos días

good morning

buenas noches

good night

por favor
please

gracias
thank you

sí
yes

no
no

la familia

the family

la madre

mom

el padre

dad

la hermana

sister

el hermano

brother

la abuela
grandma

el abuelo
grandpa

la tía
aunt

el tío
uncle

un perro
dog
los animales
the animals
un gato
cat

un pájaro
bird
un pez
fish

Lugares – Places

la casa

house

la escuela

school

el parque

park

la playa

beach

El abecedario - The Alphabet

letter	sound
A	ah
B	beh
C	seh
D	deh
E	eh
F	ehfe
G	heh
H	acheh
I	ee
J	hota
K	kah
L	eleh
M	emeh
N	eneh
Ñ	enyeh
O	oh
P	peh
Q	cu
R	ereh
S	eseh
T	teh
U	ooh
V	veh
W	dobleh veh
X	ehkees
Y	ye
Z	seta

Index

Visit **abdokids.com** to access crafts, games, videos, and more!

Use Abdo Kids code

IIK8336

or scan this QR code!